EDITOR LETTER

Mother's Day reminds us of all the Hot Moms who have appeared in Kandy over the years. We published our first Hot Moms issue in 2020. Since then, a few Kandy girls have become moms, new Kandy girls were moms, all of them shared their news on their social media pages. We welcome to motherhood and the world of KANDY Hot Moms:
- Khloe Terae
- Jennifer Irene
- Cover model Leanna Decker
- Colleen Elizabeth
- Lauren Smitty
- Trista Mikail
- Kourtney Reppert

Joining our newest Hot Moms are existing Hot Moms from 2020:
- Jessica Hall
- Rachel Bernstein
- Laurie Young

Our sports and entertainment features this month focus on documentaries and economics. First, in the world of sports where there is an unholy alliance between gambling sites, television networks and professional sports leagues. I examine the wealth discrepancy professional and collegiate sports are creating in our society. I leave no stone unturned. Our entertainment features examine a couple documentaries, The Blue Angels and The Beach Boys. Were you aware that the US government once declared that The Beach Boys attracted the wrong element? We also take a deep look at Ryan Gosling's latest film, The Fall Guy, a modern version of 1980s television hit The Fall Guy starring the Six Million Dollar Man Lee Majors. We wrap up our entertainment features with a quick glance at Furious: A Mad Max Saga, another film franchise based on a male character which is now about female empowerment. Oh boy.

We skimp on the lifestyle features this month with a single feature from our Car Guy. He takes a look at the new Mercedes-Benz CLE Cabriolet, a sporty vehicle if you are female. Guys, although he does not offer an opinion, I suggest passing unless your wife or mistress is in the market for new wheels.

Cheers!
Ron Kuchler
Editor in Chief

© Kandy Magazine 2024

CONTENTS   MAY 2024

COVER GIRL

LEANNA DECKER

We harken back to a rare Kandy double feature - a redhead and artistic images.

GIRLS

HOT MOMS 2024

This years collection of KANDY Hot Moms includes:
- Rachel Bernstein (pictured middle)
- Laurie Young
- Jessica Hall
- Jennifer Irene
- Trista Mikail
- Khloe Terae (pictured bottom left)
- Lauren Smitty (pictured below)
- Colleen Elizabeth
- Kourtney Reppert

© Kandy Magazine 2024

ARTICLES

LIFESTYLE

The CLE Cabriolet joins the recently introduced CLE Coupe and brings its own unique character, from the classic acoustic soft top to available leather seats with a special reflective coating to stay cool on the warmest days.

ENTERTAINMENT

THE FALL GUY
This film is inspired by 1980s television show of the same name, The Fall Guy starred the charismatic Lee Majors as Colt Seavers, a Hollywood stuntman doubling as a bounty hunter. The show, which was infused with thrilling stunt sequences and a good dose of humor, achieved cult classic status.

THE BEACH BOYS
"The Beach Boys" is a celebration of the legendary band that revolutionized pop music, and the iconic, harmonious sound they created that personified the California dream.

THE BLUE ANGELS
The Blue Angels also takes audiences behind the scenes for a revealing, in-depth look at what it takes to become a Blue Angel — from the careful selection process to the challenging training regimen, and on through the demanding eight-month show season.

FURIOS: A MAD MAX SAGA
All-new original, standalone action adventure that will reveal the origins of the powerhouse character.

SPORTS POTPOURRI

Outside of broadcast television, the thread that connects all the sports leagues is advertising, specifically gambling and big pharma ads. We take a close look.

© Kandy Magazine 2024

JENNIFER IRENE

© Kandy Magazine 2024

Is this the first shoot since having a kid? I did a cover for a shooting magazine and a couple other shooting magazines and also showed up on the cover of some other shooting magazine in France that I had no idea about. Somebody sent me a picture from the airport in France and I said, hey that's me. That's cool.

What was it like to step back in front of the camera for a glamour shoot? It was really nice. It was invigorating. I have been working really hard since having the baby to get my fitness back in check. It's easier said than done. It's a new life I have. I think it is inspiring to other women out there too who are afraid to embrace motherhood. You can still be sexy and beautiful and be a family woman. It was really nice.

We follow your Instagram page dedicated to Firearms training. I would call it more Tactical Training. We work with a lot of influential people in entertainment, particularly for their roles in movies or self-defense. We had the Kardashians come out; we had a chance to work with Keanu Reeves and Halle Berry for John Wick. I got to do a couple yoga poses with Halle Berry. That was really cool. She was one of the nicest people I ever met.

Did you take a selfie with Halle Berry? I did. I pinned a few of them on my Instagram where I was doing yoga with Halle.

Photos Chaz
HMU Jennifer Irene

| KANDY | CAR GUY |

2024 MERCEDES-BENZ CLE CABRIOLET

The breathtaking CLE Cabriolet is the latest four-seat, open-top dream car from Mercedes-Benz.

Starting at $64,350, the 2024 CLE Cabriolet combines dynamic driving enjoyment with everyday comfort

HIGHLIGHTS
- Extensive standard equipment with AIRCAP®, AIRSCARF®, Burmester® 3D Surround Sound System and third generation MBUX infotainment
- Smooth, powerful 48-volt mild hybrid engines
- Sophisticated aerodynamics for optimized comfort and aeroacoustics
- First Mercedes-Benz Cabriolet with separate head airbag for rear passengers as standard

US MSRP Trim levels
- CLE 300 4MATIC Cabriolet: $64,350
- CLE 450 4MATIC Cabriolet: $73,850
- CLE 300 4MATIC Cabriolet: $66,950
- CLE 450 4MATIC Cabriolet: $76,450

The CLE Cabriolet joins the recently introduced CLE Coupe and brings its own unique character, from the classic acoustic soft top to available leather seats with a special reflective coating to stay cool on the warmest days. The Cabriolet features extensive standard equipment, including the AIRCAP® electric wind deflector system, AIRSCARF®, Burmester® 3D Surround Sound, third generation Mercedes-Benz User Experience (MBUX) infotainment and more.

Thanks to a 1-inch longer wheelbase, the CLE Cabriolet is significantly more spacious than the previous C- Class Cabriolet.

© Kandy Magazine 2024

Rear passengers benefit from 0.6-inches more leg room, 0.9-inches more shoulder room and 0.7-inches more elbow room. The trunk features 13.6 cubic feet of space when the soft top is up, 10.4 cubic feet with top down. Cargo space can be increased by deploying the 60:40 split folding rear seat backrests.

Exterior design
Like the CLE Coupe, the CLE Cabriolet features a powerful, athletic exterior – from the aerodynamic "shark nose" front end to the seamless rear design. The forward-leaning front end with low-slung hood and unique flat LED headlights lead to a newly designed, three-dimensional chrome grille with a Mercedes-Benz pattern. A highlight at the rear of the vehicle is the two-part LED taillights with new contours and three-dimensional light bodies.

The AMG Line package (optional on CLE 300 4MATIC, standard on CLE 450 4MATIC) adds AMG exterior design elements and performance equipment ranging from larger brake discs on the front axle to an AMG front bumper with sport air intakes and chrome trim elements, as well as an exhaust system with two visible tailpipe trim elements integrated into the bumper and sporty engine sound.

The package also introduces a number of distinctive interior elements including, a multifunction sports steering wheel in Nappa leather wIth horizontal twin-spokes and flat bottom, AMG brushed stainless steel sports pedals with black rubber studs, climate control vents with silver chrome accents, door trim in high-gloss black with silver chrome accents, among other unique details.

Further personalization to the CLE Cabriolet is available with the Night Package, an array of exterior paints, including four new MANUFACTURER colors, as well as a variety of wheels in sizes up to 20-inches.
First Mercedes-Benz Cabriolet with separate head airbag for rear passengers

The reinforced bodyshell structures gives the CLE Cabriolet a high level of structural safety, even without a fixed roof. The standard safety equipment includes 11 airbags with a new center airbag between the two front seats and, for the first time in a Mercedes-Benz Cabriolet, a head protection system with two separate head airbags for the rear passengers.

Among the numerous advanced driver assistance systems on the CLE Cabriolet:
- Blind Spot Assist,
- Active Brake Assist
- ATTENTION ASSIST

The available Driver Assistance Package offers expanded functionality
- Active Lane Change Assist
- DISTRONIC PLUS with Steering Assist
- Stop & Go Assist, Route-Based Speed Adaptation

© Kandy Magazine 2024

KANDY **COVER MODEL**

LEANNA DECKER

Choosing a cover girl for our HOT Mom's issue is a laborious task. There are so many KANDY Hot Moms! For 2024, we harken back to a rare Kandy double feature - a redhead and artistic images.

Why should men marry a southern girl? Well, we have manners which is a plus {laughs}. Also, we know how to get down and dirty, as well as dress up and be classy.

What is the most amazing thing about your hometown? My hometown is a very tiny quaint town in Kentucky. I love coming home; it's quiet and the people are so friendly. There really is no place like home :)

What trait of Virgos is your best match? I'm very hardworking and positive which I feel are two of my strongest Virgo traits.

Out of curiosity, who would you say is your all-time favorite redhead. Not to be conceited but me {Smiles}. You have to love yourself, of course!

Any special talents? My talents go down in the kitchen. I love food and cooking! I love mixing flavors then watching my guests have mini mouthgasms when eating my food. Ha-ha

Seduce us in the kitchen. What are you going to whip up? Well, for starters, we will have a fresh garden salad then some yummy homemade meatloaf with mashed potatoes and sweet corn! My specialty.

Photos by Volker
Makeup by Natalie Rose
Hair Alex Thao
Stylist Jen Summers

Follow Leanna online
Instagram @leannadecker
X @leanna_decker
Facebook- officialleannadecker

© Kandy Magazine 2024

LAUREN SMITY

© Kandy Magazine 2024

Tell us about your dog walker business. I started my company Social Canines 3 years ago. Dogs have always been a huge part of my life and bring me so much joy. I wanted to give back and help them have happier and healthier lives. It is pack walks, so I take about 10 dogs out on a 2-hour hike. It is the best job in the world!

How many pups can you walk at once? Most I've walked was 15 by myself.

What is the best advice you can give to fellow dog owners? It's so important to build trust and a friendship between you and your dog. They are always watching you and learning from your behavior and the energy you give off. If you lead them confidently, instead of acting superior to them, they learn much more efficiently. And always be consistent in training them to do or not to do something.

What is the billboard we noticed on your Instagram page? I shot a GUESS campaign where they launched their first GUESS Sport x Pleasures line. The billboard was in Beverly Hills.

Photos Mike Prado

Sports Potpourri

By Ron Kuchler

This issue, a look at US sports economics impact on viewers and the NFL draft changes.

Outside of broadcast television, the thread that connects all US sports leagues is advertising, specifically gambling and big pharma ads. The targeting of American consumers, with a propensity to addiction, has reached pandemic levels via gambling and big pharma advertising. Sports networks and leagues are now in bed with gambling sites, inflicting deep consumer pain. ESPN and Penn have partnered in a new ESPN-branded gambling site. MSG networks feature celebrity athletes to promote a gambling partnership with Caesars. The NHL employs rink board digital ads to promote big pharma.

It is bad enough the American middle class has been squeezed by the government's propensity to give money to foreign nations and non-US citizens, but for the sports complex to pillage the pockets of their revenue bread and butter base is outrageous. Our hope is league commissioners awaken, have an epiphany, and realize the moral depravity of what they are inflicting on fans.

The NFL draft has runneth over its banks. What do we mean? Point one. Why is the national anthem played at a draft? Why is a single demographic catered with their own anthem? We are all Americans. There is one anthem for this country. And there is no need to play the anthem at a draft.

Point two. We missed the humbleness of the draft, once held in a tiny ballroom in New York City. For what must have been the tenth time, I recently watched the ESPN 30 for 30 documentary Elway to Marino. As commissioner Pete Rozell took to the podium time after time to announce a team's pick, you could sense the intimacy in the room that connected the league to the fans and the fans to the teams. That intimacy has long disappeared.

Point three. We understand the human interests story the networks are attempting to craft with the green room and the cameras in the homes of NFL draftees. However, the average Joe watching the draft on television will never earn in his lifetime what most of these draftees will earn from their initial rookie contract. When Pete Rozelle was commissioner, we celebrated the drafting of college kids as we could relate. Today, we cannot relate to these players earning millions of dollars. The fans with a smidgen of common sense realize that it is their hard-earned dollars that are paying these players million-dollar salaries through outrageous cable and streaming fees, inflated sneaker prices, everyday male hygiene items like razors, deodorant and shampoo, a weekend six-pack of their favorite beer, and everything else that makes us men. The consumer is held hostage by the NFL and their corporate sponsors.

The enjoyment of the NFL is no longer measurable. Whether you choose cable, satellite, or a streaming service for your entertainment, you are hostage to the cost of professional and now collegiate sports. The fees sports and entertainment conglomerates pay to these leagues to televise their product to an American audience burden us all – the 80-year-old grandmother on a fixed income, the struggling middle-class family with two working parents who can barely afford to feed and clothe their kids, the college graduate who spends 50% of his net pay on student loan payments. Whether you are a sports fan or not, you pay so that professional athletes and college students may earn millions playing a game. Unless you are a millionaire or a billionaire, there is a reasonable cost to enjoy sporting events, a cost that crossed the Rubicon a long time ago.

© Kandy Magazine 2024

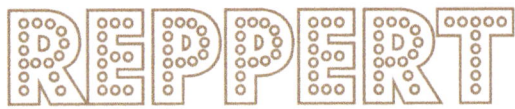
KOURTNEY REPPERT

Does Kourtney look familiar? Kourtney and KANDY go back to our KANDY Hollywood parties days. Or her Jessica Simpson resemblance may have had you pondering where you've seen her.

For our fans who don't know, remind everyone of your hometown. From small town Leesport PA! Born and raised in country town!

Imagine a zombie apocalypse wipes all the men off the planet except Amish and Pennsylvania Dutch men. Who did you marry and why? A real cowboy. They know how to survive, and they take care of their ladies!

When was the first time someone said you resembled Jessica Simpson? I was in middle school when her album Sweet Kisses came out, that kind of started it all! I never imagined one day in the future I would meet her and be her stand in and work for her. She really helped inspire me to become the best I could be! **Wow! That's amazing. We recall all the fame you were receiving from the resemblance, but we did not know the entire backstory. How incredible!**

Name your favorite restaurant in America. Sloppy Joe's in Key West! Best oysters in town and conch fritters! You gotta' try! **We love that place! The drinks and live music ain't too bad either!**

Describe a hidden talent of yours. I am super tech savvy. Not many people know that. I love being underestimated.

Photos by Mike Prado
Makeup Stephanie Kilmer
Hair by Zoe Carpenter

© Kandy Magazine 2024

© Kandy Magazine 2024

TRISTA MIKAIL

When these images of Trista appeared in our Dropbox, we knew immediately we had found the perfect LOOK to celebrate Motherhood KANDY style.

As we celebrate Hot Moms this month, we also are celebrating Life. And what better way to celebrate Life than with a beautiful woman who is sharing her pregnancy with 450,000 loyal fans.

Most men's magazines will hide the fact that a model is pregnant. And practically every men's magazine will shy away from publishing a model who is pregnant. Not KANDY.

If you have been a long-time reader of KANDY, you know we love to challenge the status quo.

A quick trip to Trista's Instagram account @tristamikail and you'll see Trista in all her pregnancy majesty. Childbirth is a natural feature of being a woman. We say celebrate womanhood and the birth of a new life.

Photo Ashlee K. AJK Photography
PR LSA Models

© Kandy Magazine 2024

CELEBRITY | FEATURE

THE REAL FALL GUY'S STORY: DAVID LEITCH
Courtesy Universal Pictures

Photos Eric Laciste/Universal Pictures, Copyright: © Universal Studios. All Rights

In the electrifying realm of action filmmaking, where daring stunts and adrenaline-fueled sequences reign supreme, few possess the firsthand experience and unique perspective that Fall Guy director David Leitch brings to the table. Transitioning from his roots as a stunt performer, Leitch has become a luminary in the industry, seamlessly blending gripping narratives with high-octane action.

Leitch's early days in the industry were marked by years of hard work and determination as he honed his skills behind the scenes before transitioning into directing. A pivotal moment in Leitch's career was working as Brad Pitt's stunt double on Fight Club, which offered a front-row seat to observe director David Fincher's meticulous approach to filmmaking.

"As a stunt performer, I had the privilege of watching and learning without anyone rushing me off the set," Leitch says.

"When I saw Fincher work, I became hooked on the filmmaking process. As I continued my stunt career, I began my own filmmaking journey on the side. I filmed shorts, edited them and focused on choreographing, shooting and presenting action sequences as cohesive stories to directors. This was my transition from performing stunts to designing action and choreography."

But Leitch's aspirations went beyond choreography. "I wanted to direct," Leitch says. "The opportunities to shoot major action sequences as a second-unit director started coming my way, but I knew I had to keep pushing for that goal of directing a full feature. The moment came with John Wick."

© Kandy Magazine 2024

Although the official director credit for John Wick was attributed to Chad Stahelski per the Director's Guild guidelines, it is widely acknowledged that Leitch directed the film alongside Stahelski. Since then, Leitch has directed global box office smash-hits Bullet Train, Fast & Furious Presents: Hobbs & Shaw, Deadpool 2 and Atomic Blonde.

Despite his directorial success, Leitch remains deeply connected to his roots.

"My career is built on 20 years of being a stunt performer, taking hits, riding wires, crashing cars, being set on fire and working closely with every department in the industry," Leitch says.

"My love for moviemaking kept me going. I learned the film production model inside and out through years of working with various departments. If you asked me to stop directing movies and go back to being a stunt coordinator, I'd still be thrilled because there's no place I'd rather be than on a movie set, making art with my friends."

The term 'fall guy' has a rich history in the stunt world, originally referring to the performers who take physical hits for the sake of creating cinematic magic.

"They're the ones falling off horses, bikes or down a set of stairs," Leitch says. "But in our film, we've given this term a broader meaning. It's evolved into a metaphor that we use in various ways. Our fall guy is not just a stuntman taking falls for the camera; he's someone unfairly taking the blame for something he didn't do. He's also a man who's fallen deeply in love, willing to risk it all to reclaim the love of his life."

And for Leitch, The Fall Guy is much more than a filmmaking endeavor.

"The Fall Guy, to me, is truly a love letter to stunt performers and the unsung heroes of the film industry—the highly skilled and talented artisans who contribute their passion and dedication to the art of moviemaking," Leitch says. "It's a tribute to the production designers, cinematographers, grips, electrics, PAs, ADs, and everyone in between who pours their hearts and souls into crafting the magic of storytelling on screen. This project holds a special place in my heart because it weaves in real-life anecdotes from my journey as a stunt performer and a part of the crew."

© Kandy Magazine 2024

THE FALL GUY

Genre: Action Thriller
Release Date: May 3rd
Starring: Ryan Gosling, Emily Blunt, Winston Duke, Aaron Taylor-Johnson, Hannah Waddingham, Stephanie Hsu
Directed by: David Leitch
Studio: Universal

The Fall Guy is a big screen adaptation of real-life stunt man and director David Leitch. A new hilarious, hard-driving, all-star apex-action thriller and love letter to action movies and the hard-working and under-appreciated crew of people who make them: The Fall Guy.

Studio Synopsis
Over the course of ten days and 435 miles, an unHe's a stuntman, and like everyone in the stunt community, he gets blown up, shot, crashed, thrown through windows and dropped from the highest of heights, all for our entertainment. And now, fresh off an almost career-ending accident, this working-class hero has to track down a missing movie star, solve a conspiracy and try to win back the love of his life while still doing his day job. What could possibly go right?

In this modern adaptation, Ryan Gosling (The Big Short, La La Land, Drive) stars as Colt Seavers, a battle-scarred stuntman who, having left the business a year earlier to focus on both his physical and mental health, is drafted back into service when the star of a mega-budget studio movie—being directed by his ex, Jody Moreno, played by Emily Blunt (Oppenheimer, A Quiet Place films, Sicario)—goes missing.

While the film's ruthless producer, maneuvers to keep the disappearance of star Tom Ryder a secret from the studio and the media, Colt performs the film's most outrageous stunts while trying (with limited success) to charm his way back into Jody's good graces. But as the mystery around the missing star deepens, Colt will find himself ensnared in a sinister, criminal plot that will push him to the edge of a fall more dangerous than any stunt.

Kandy Says
We love all the advance features put out by the studio. We are big fans of the original Fall Guy from the 1980s. We say two thumbs up to The Fall Guy and we look forward to the sequels and spin-offs.

Did you know...
This film is inspired by 1980s television show of the same name, The Fall Guy starred the charismatic Lee Majors as Colt Seavers, a Hollywood stuntman doubling as a bounty hunter. The show, which was infused with thrilling stunt sequences and a good dose of humor, achieved cult classic status and earned substantial success across its five-season run. Alongside Majors, the show's other main characters included Heather Thomas as Jody Banks, a fellow stunt performer, and Douglas Barr as Howie Munson, Colt's affable and tech-savvy sidekick and cousin.

© Kandy Magazine 2024

KANDY   MOVIES

Photo Credit Bobby Baldock

THE BLUE ANGELS
Category: Documentary
Studio: Amazon MGM Studio
Directed By Paul Crowder
Photos © Amazon Content Services LLC

Studio Synopsis
The Blue Angels have been enthralling crowds—across the country and around the globe — for more than 75 years. Now, the brand new documentary The Blue Angels will take audiences soaring with the Navy's elite Flight Demonstration Squadron as never before. Filmed for IMAX®, the immersive footage puts you in the cockpit for a firsthand view of the Blue Angels' precision flying, while the aerial shots deliver a spectacular showcase of the breathtaking maneuvers that have made them the world's premier jet team.

The Blue Angels also takes audiences behind the scenes for a revealing, in-depth look at what it takes to become a Blue Angel — from the careful selection process to the challenging training regimen, and on through the demanding eight-month show season. The film is a fitting tribute to the extraordinary teamwork, passion and pride of the hundreds of outstanding men and women of the Navy and Marine Corps who have had the honor to serve in the Blue Angels...past, present and future.

Kandy Says
In lieu of what Kandy Says, we turn this over to the filmmakers whom echo our immeasurable respect for The Blue Angels.

Every year, millions of people are wowed by the daring aerobatic maneuvers of the United States Navy Blue Angels. For generations, fans have flocked to air shows from coast to coast, cheering as the iconic blue and gold jets take to the skies in a dynamic demonstration of power and precision that pushes the envelope of what man and machine can do. The tight Blue Angel Diamond and the high-performance Solos take turns thrilling the crowds until all six jets come together for the trademark Delta formation. However, since their inception in 1946, few people outside of the organization have been allowed behind the scenes to see everything that goes into putting together a Blue Angels season. Until now.

© Kandy Magazine 2024

Photo Credit Rob Stone

KANDYMAG.COM | MAY 2024

KANDY MOVIES

The Beach Boys

(L-R) Dennis Wilson, Al Jardine, Carl Wilson, Brian Wilson, Mike Love. Circa 1964
(Photo Michael Ochs Archives/Getty Images)

Category: Music Documentary
Rating: PG-13
Where: Disney+
Directed by: Frank Marshall, Thom Zimny
Interviewees: Brian Wilson, Mike Love, Carl Wilson, Dennis Wilson, Al Jardine, David Marks, Bruce Johnston, Josh Kun, Don Was, Ryan Tedder, Marilyn Wilson-Rutherford, Lindsey Buckingham, Don Randi, Janelle Monáe, Blondie Chaplin

Kandy Says
The Beach Boys personified the good life. As a senior in high school, we experienced a Senior School Trip to Six Flags Great Adventure in New Jersey. The original Beach Boys were the featured musical guests that evening at the amusement park. It was the perfect ending to a great day of teen celebration.

Studio Synopsis
"The Beach Boys" is a celebration of the legendary band that revolutionized pop music, and the iconic, harmonious sound they created that personified the California dream, captivating fans for generations and generations to come.

The documentary traces the band from humble family beginnings and features never-before-seen footage and all-new interviews with The Beach Boys' Brian Wilson, Mike Love, Al Jardine, David Marks, Bruce Johnston, plus other luminaries in the music business, including Lindsey Buckingham, Janelle Monae, Ryan Tedder, and Don Was. Viewers will also hear from the group's Carl and Dennis Wilson in their own words.

Did You Know... President Reagan's Secretary of Interior once banned The Beach Boys from playing on the 4th of July on the National Mall. Secretary Watt claimed the Beach Boys attracted the wrong element.

© Kandy Magazine 2024

KANDY MOVIES

FURIOSA: A MAD MAX SAGA
Genre: Sci-fi
Rating: R
Starring: Anya Taylor-Joy, Chris Hemsworth
Director: George Miller
Studios: Warner Bros.

Studio Synopsis
"Furiosa: A Mad Max Saga," the much-anticipated return to the iconic dystopian world Miller created more than 40 years ago with the seminal "Mad Max" films. Miller now turns the page again with an all-new original, stand-alone action adventure that will reveal the origins of the powerhouse character from "Mad Max: Fury Road."

As the world fell, young Furiosa is snatched from the Green Place of Many Mothers and falls into the hands of a great Biker Horde led by the Warlord Dementus. Sweeping through the Wasteland, they come across the Citadel presided over by The Immortan Joe. While the two Tyrants war for dominance, Furiosa must survive many trials as she puts together the means to find her way home.

Kandy Says
The Road Warrior. Mad Max. Mad Max Beyond Thunderdome. Mad Max: Fury Road. As we wrote in a previous issue about the Godzilla 60s and 70s films, the franchise may have run its course. The studio has different ideas. As was the case with Mad Max: Fury Road, Furiosa is about female empowerment with the storyline centered around the character Furiosa. How about we return to the namesake character the franchise is built upon?

RACHEL BERNSTEIN

As one of the most beautiful women to grace the pages of KANDY magazine, and one of the most beautiful women in the world, Rachel holds a very special place in our KANDY hearts. She is sweet as she is beautiful. She is classy as she is sexy. She is kind as she is intelligent.

Rachel, her modeling and personal social media brand is 'Sunset Blonde', introduced the world to Cashmere Hair, her hair extensions product line, on Shark Tank. Fast forward a couple years, Rachel and her husband, with kids in tow, move to the greener pastures of San Diego from Los Angeles.

As a business owner and mom, would you say your fan base on social media has changed? Yes, I think, as soon as I started posting about my pregnancy, my fan base changed a lot. But now I feel I have many amazing women that follow my journey.

How would you say your children have reshaped your life? Having children changed my life in so many ways. I don't even live the same life. I moved out of Los Angeles to San Diego to give my kids a better life. I spend many hours caring for my kids, teaching my kids, and traveling with my kids. My life is filled with doing things with my family, which is the thing that brings me the most happiness every day. Love is everything.

Photos Mike Prado
HMU Sunset Blonde

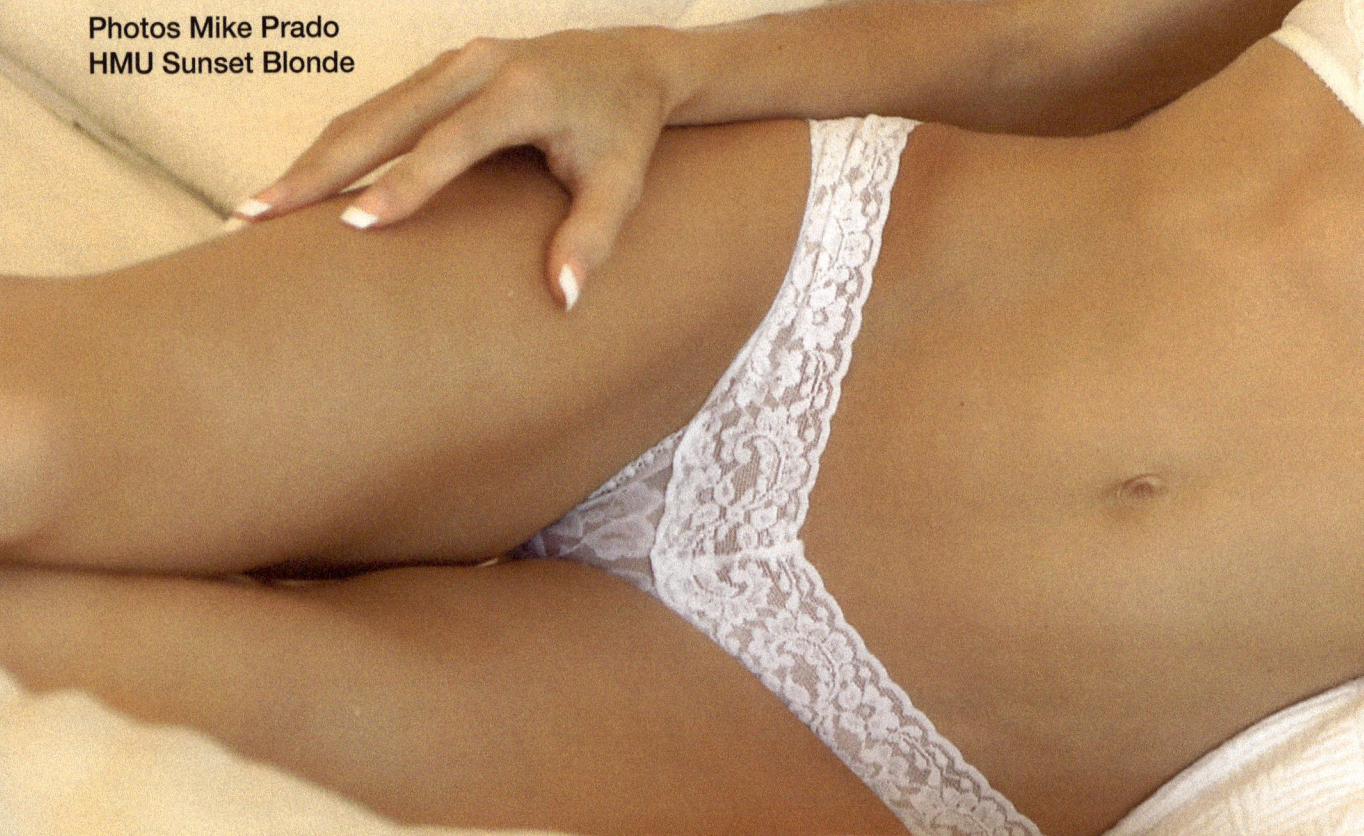

© Kandy Magazine 2024

Laurie share with our readers your shoot overview. "I'm still hot!!! Ha ha ha That was my initial thought. Like wow! Zero editing and I still got it. I guess after having two kids and being locked away because of the state of the world for 2 years, I didn't know if I'd ever model again. And I certainly didn't feel hot anymore in my sweats and mask. But this gave me the confidence to realize I can keep doing this job that I love so much. It's really been a self-esteem boost seeing these photos!

We weren't excited about the choice of the orange bikini. I mean, it is an orange bikini, but did you ever put sizzle into that orange. Ahh, I love it! The orange was honestly (because when we initially spoke about styling) I wanted a lack of color, boho theme, but you wanted some pops of color and I saw this and I thought… ooh orange! And gosh… those earrings really pop.

We had our difference of opinion. But we finally got our way. You always do, but it was a great compromise, and the orange was such a great color out there on the beach.

© Kandy Magazine 2024

JESSICA HALL

Hello Jessica. Welcome back to Kandy. It's good to be back here in Kandy land. Can I say that or is that trademarked? Let's just say it. It works. I absolutely love that Ron reached out to me and wanted me to shoot again for Kandy magazine. I couldn't be more excited just to be a part of something I've loved from day one. The fact that I am here now just with everything I've done. Ron let me have kind of my idea of what's going on in my life and just let it portray through the pictures that we took today. It's called Jessica in Charge; a lot of these Kandy girls have done so much, and it is so cool that Ron sees that… wants us to talk about our story… wants to show it through photos. That's a really cool thing about Kandy magazine, the loyalty. It's always so classy; you know what you are going to get.

What shall we talk about Jessica? I'm an open book and will answer anything.

You said to me one-time that you would try anything once. Hey! I don't want to regret anything, so yes, I'll try almost anything. There are a few things I'll never do again such as multiple shots of tequila or sky jumping. I know two totally different things, but both made me super nauseous.

What is your expectation fan base to your newest Kandy feature? I think they will love it! It's been a while since I showed some skin. I mean I'm going from a baby belly to push up bras. I love that Kandy loves every age in women and appreciates all body types. I'm proud at this age, with 2 kids… I hope I make Kandy proud.

Photos Mario Barberio
HMU Sara Cranham
Stylist Julia Perry

© Kandy Magazine 2024

© Kandy Magazine 2024

Editor in Chief
Ron Kuchler

Managing Editor
David Packo

Associate Editor
Steve Scala

Director of Marketing
Bill Nychay

COVER PHOTOGRAPHER
VOLKER FLECK

CONTRIBUTORS
Mario Barberio, Visual Poison, Tropic Pic, Aaron Riveroll
Mike Prado, Chaz, AJK Photography,

Contact Us
Kandy Enterprises LLC
7260 W Azure Dr. Ste 140-639
Las Vegas, NV 89130
www.kandymag.com
facebook @kandymagazine
X @kandy_magazine
instagram @kandymagazine

General Inquiries - support@kandymag.com
Letters to The Editor - letters@kandymag.com
Copyright - legal@kandymag.com
Subscriptions - subscriptions@kandymag.com

HOT MOMS 2024
© 2024 Kandy Enterprises LLC.
All Rights Reserved.

INSIDE COVER

LEFT BLANK

INTENTIONALLY

www.ingramcontent.com/pod-product-compliance
Lightning Source LLC
LaVergne TN
LVHW072122060526
838201LV00068B/4955